LOOKING WESTWA

Published by Truran, Croft Prince, Mount Hawke,
Truro, Cornwall. TR48EE.   www.truranbooks.co.uk
Printed by R. Booth at the Troutbeck Press,
Antron Hill, Mabe, Penryn, Cornwall. TR109HH

ISBN   1   85022   157   X   (cased)
ISBN   1   85022   158   8   (paperback)

For me, this is the best part of Cornwall – the high ground of West Penwith. Rarely out of sight of the sea, bleak, beautiful, open & empty. Larks singing & buzzards calling. And all around, the evidence of the continuity of life here, from the Bronze age to the miners & labourers of the last few centuries & the farmers of today, still using the fields & sometimes the homesteads of ancient days......

3

leaving St. Ives ...
looking back...

... & forward.

SLOW

4

with the sea on the right - all the way to Lands End.

The first big hill out of St Ives. Very blowy.
Walkers & riders passing. The base of the
road loops around hills & seems to form a barrier between
moorland on the left & flat farmland on the right.
Far too windy to sit here for very long.

6

I'm off to find a cup of coffee in zennor* — And found a very good one!
*

Zennor – houses clustered
round the church, surrounded
by fields that have probably
been the same for thousands
of years. Always quiet.
Had to visit the mermaid in
the church – as always...
Sheltered & warm here away
from the wind . . .

8

9

on the road between St Ives & Zennor

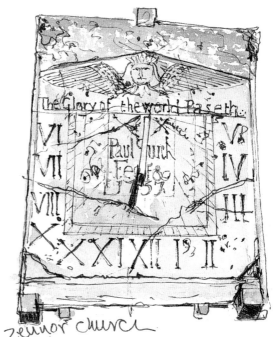

The Glory of the world Passeth

Paul Church 1597

zennor church

in the middle of nowhere!

CREAM TEAS
B + B at
MANOR FARM
near the
LIGHTHOUSE!

As I watch blue light from the stained glass falls across the mermaid.

Zennor

Asleep in the Wayside Museum

Boswednack I think.

11

The road weaves between small farms r hamlets
r is not made for cars . . . .

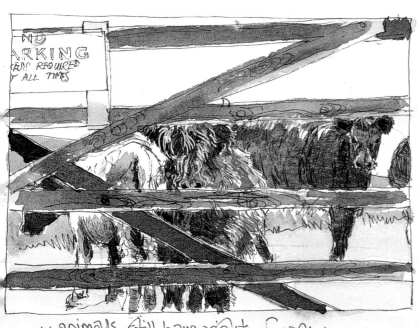

.. animals still have right of way ..

I'm not sure what kind of ram this is, but he saw his little flock across the road, turned, glared at me ·· r was gone'.

13

The farrier, parked in the road outside a barn...

A rubbing stone for the cows? or a standing stone?

Porthmeor Farm sheltering under the bare ridge of Carn Galver.

I've always loved these old buildings where the
road curves through the farm yard.
There's usually something in the road - a
sleeping dog, hens, geese - r sometimes
guinea fowl!

15

16

these cottages on the road just before Morvah are called 'Waterloo' - I've often wondered why?...

18

There is a buzzard standing in this field who looks like he's stalking. He's ungainly on the ground ... rather than walk. He seems to hop ... whole time I've been there. He ... they are much more elegant in the air.

19

20

sheltering from the rain in the schoolhouse Gallery in Morvah.
creamy pink light under heavy cloud
Pendeen dark on the horizon. Huge dark clouds blowing in
from the sea.

21

morvah, with the
wonderful walls on the left
They're built quite differently to
anywhere else & I imagine
one farmer, years ago,
building them all

And the red phone phone box which stands out like a beacon - r once gave you all your money back for months! There used to be a queue waiting to use it ·· ··

23

Lanyon

Men an Tol

24

chûn

chûn castle is the centre of west Penwith for me. once I'm inside the walls, I know I'm safe....

I always feel I should ask permission to enter these gates — so I do..

25

Pendeen lighthouse... - years ago, when we lived in Pendeen, I used to lay awake on foggy nights listening to the foghorn & counting the seconds. I think it was three blasts & then 20 seconds quiet... We sold our pony to the lighthouse keeper & she lived right here in this field. She became so used to the noise that she didn't appear to hear it at all... And there's a lot of fog at Pendeen!

Looking back to Pendeen from the lighthouse road. Rows of
terraced cottages. No trees. Bleak & open country . . . Beautiful . . 27

Terraced cottages at Carngoath

28

I don't think architects can design houses so pleasing to the eye as these.

29

A detour off the road at Botallack, the cliff path winds past engine houses, waste heaps + chimneys

30

These two are the most romantic-looking ruins now, & it must
have been such hell to work there...

31

32

33

St. Just spreads out from the
church & Plain an Gwarry.
It's low built & grey,
solid & ancient.

And still a good, honest
working town.
It has seen good times &
bad – & looks as if it will
survive plenty more of
both.

My daughters went to school here
& now my grandaughter does – one of the best of places..

35

TO
SAINT JUST
3
MICOS

TO
PENZANCE
5½
MILES.

TO
LAND'S END
4½
MILES.

Both sides of a granite stone at Crows an wra
witches cross I think it means – and the
cross is right next to the stone

TO
ST BURYAN
3
MILES
AD 1830

TO
LANDS END
4
MILES
TO
S JUST
2 MI

As you come down the road from Crows an wra these signs are at the bottom. Behind them the airfield stretches away flat & the fields drop into the sea

The road goes past Lands End Aerodrome
A place I know well, with many an hour spent waiting for
the fog to clear so that the plane could fly home to Scilly.
crows & seagulls battling into the wind
Squalls passing over, skybus revs up & goes across the field at about
the speed you could drive it — & somehow manages to take off —
38 I've always thought that it only does, because everyone breathes
in sharply just before the edge
of the field

39

You can always tell which way is west . . .

41

Walked to the top of Chapel Carn Brea - the most westerly hill in Britain. Its flat-topped, conical shape rises with steep sides from the flat fields all round. . . . 360° views . . . . A Bronze age cairn on the very top - if I were an ancient chieften I'd be buried here - its a very special place. There was also a medieval chapel here & its associated beacon is still lit every midsummer eve. The nearest beacon to the west would have been on Chapel Down, St. Martins. I can't see the islands today, but sometimes they are so clear that I can see the white sand on Great Bay - (& feel homesick! . . .)

Lands End

The Longships

Sennen Cove

Sennen Churchtown

larks singing & a buzzard circling slowly over the fields
- otherwise all is still & quiet.

Escalls chapel, sitting under chapel carn Brea – a hill which always seems dark & brooding... A strong presence – even on a bright & sunny day.

45

Sennen church - next to the First & Last Inn .. Most of the churches are
next to the pub .. zennor, Pendeen, St Just - all very close — only
Morvah is without — & I think Merthyr farm, there, may once have
been one . . . .

46

This scene shows just how flat the farmland is in the narrow strip between sea & moorland hills.

Stopped to look at the church in Sennen & this is the view back up the coast, across Whitesands Bay to Cape Cornwall on a sunny February day.

47

Lands End . .

All I can see looking westward now is the horizon . . . .
r the little smudge in the distance , which is home . . .